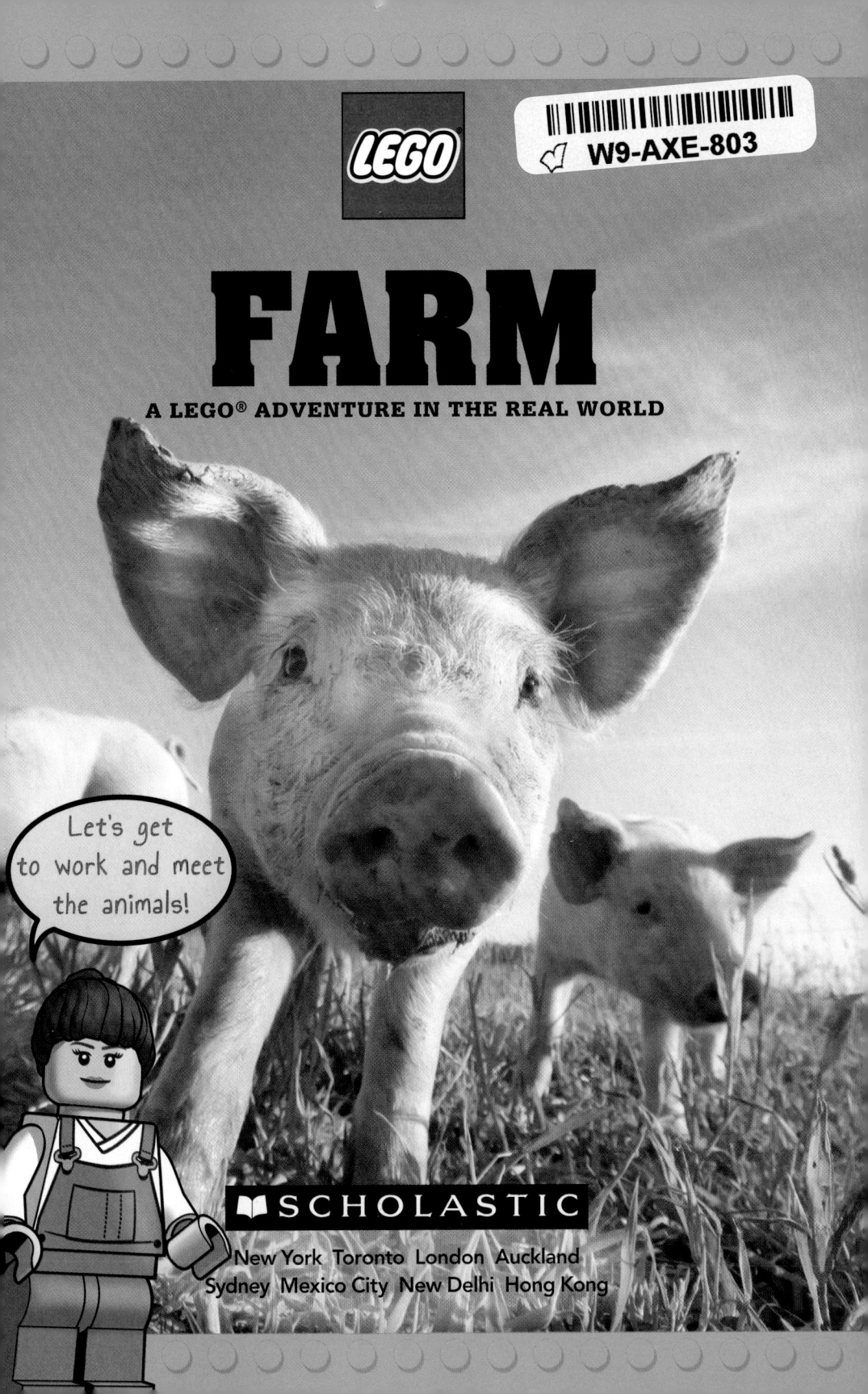

W9-AXE-803

FARM

A LEGO® ADVENTURE IN THE REAL WORLD

Let's get to work and meet the animals!

SCHOLASTIC
New York Toronto London Auckland
Sydney Mexico City New Delhi Hong Kong

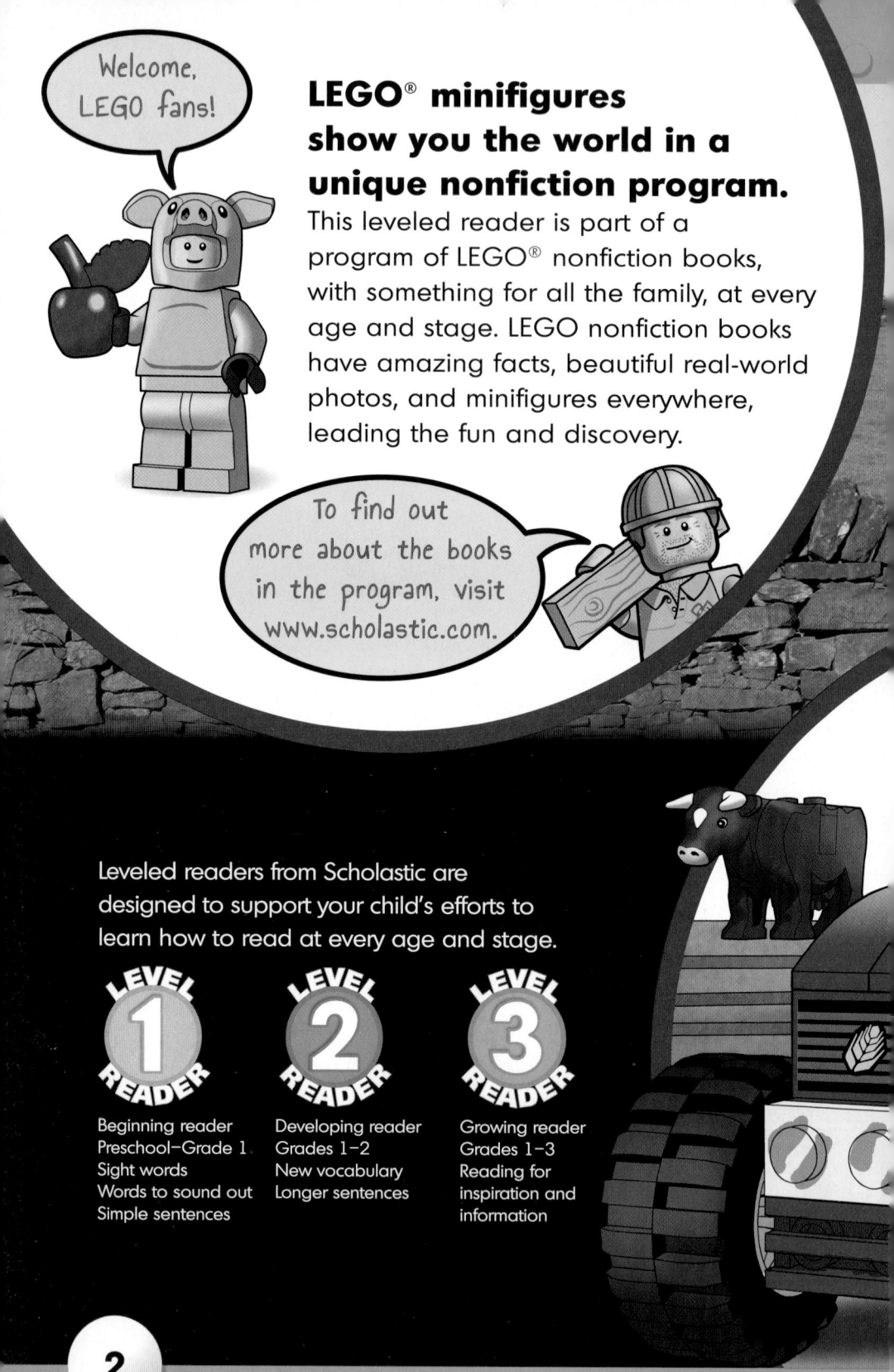

LEGO® minifigures show you the world in a unique nonfiction program.

This leveled reader is part of a program of LEGO® nonfiction books, with something for all the family, at every age and stage. LEGO nonfiction books have amazing facts, beautiful real-world photos, and minifigures everywhere, leading the fun and discovery.

Leveled readers from Scholastic are designed to support your child's efforts to learn how to read at every age and stage.

LEVEL 1 READER
Beginning reader
Preschool–Grade 1
Sight words
Words to sound out
Simple sentences

LEVEL 2 READER
Developing reader
Grades 1–2
New vocabulary
Longer sentences

LEVEL 3 READER
Growing reader
Grades 1–3
Reading for inspiration and information

BUILD IT!
Check out the epic building ideas when you see me.
Hey! Can I have a ride? I need to get to the end of this book!

It's morning on the farm.
What's happening today?
Let's hop on the tractor and
explore. Who's in the barn?

Farms are busy places, with animals to feed and crops to grow.

BUILD IT!

Create your own farm. You'll need a house to live in and a barn for your animals to sleep in.

Cluck, cluck! Let's go to the chicken coop. The chicken has laid an egg! She lays four or five eggs a week—that's about 200 per year.

She's a busy bird!
One trillion eggs are eaten each year in the world. I like mine sunny-side up!
I always have mine scrambled!

Oink, oink! These little piglets are hungry! The mommy pig, or sow, feeds milk to her piglets. Pigs are really smart. They talk to each other using grunts and squeals.

Phew, it's hot today! I need to cool down.

Here! I'll help you. Pigs keep cool by rolling in mud.

Well, I'm cool, but now I need a shower . . .

It's milking time on the dairy farm. Milk keeps our bones and teeth strong.
In Russia, people used to drop a frog in a bucket of milk to keep it fresh.
Ribbit!

One cow can produce over 80 glasses of milk a day! That's a-moo-zing!
BUILD IT!
Build a huge tanker truck to keep the milk cool and take it to supermarkets.
The biggest milkshake ever was made in a tanker truck. It made 50,000 drinks!
Tara
11

Big animal farms are called ranches. This one has more than 1,000 cows. Cowboys and cowgirls use horses to round them up.

Cowboys and cowgirls use lassos to catch cows.

Yee-haw! Watch this. Bull's-eye!

Yikes! I think I need a bit more practice . . .

Watch the cute baby lambs leaping and bouncing in the field. Lambs can walk when they are a few minutes old.

They have thick woolly fleeces to keep them warm.

BUILD IT!

Build a barn for your sheep to sleep in when it's cold. Make it warm and cozy!

The lambs are all grown up and their fleeces are long and shaggy. Phew! It's too hot. It's time for a haircut.

A sheepdog herds the sheep together. The farmer cuts the fleece. The fleece is then turned into wool.

Only a tractor can drive across bumpy, muddy fields. Huge wheels with knobby tires help grip the ground. Hold on tight, it's a bumpy ride!

Woohoo! This car is FAST! Race you across the field!
This is the easiest race I've ever won!
Uh-oh, I guess I'm stuck in second place.
The biggest tractor tire is 58 LEGO minifigures high!

Tractors aren't fast, but they pull all kinds of useful farm machines. Plows make the soil ready for crops.

Sprayers water crops. Balers collect crops in neat bundles.

BUILD IT!

Build a tractor and a farm machine for it to pull. Don't get stuck in the mud!

Most of the plants you eat, such as wheat, rice, fruit, and vegetables grow on farms. These plants are called crops.

Chocolate is made from cacao beans. They are farmed in rain forests
Sweet! I'd love to be a chocolate farmer!

It's harvest time! Grain crops, such as wheat, need to be cut when they're ripe. A combine harvester cuts the crops and then removes the seeds (grain), the part we eat.

Combine harvesters cut at 7 miles per hour (11 km/h), but they do lots of jobs at once!
BUILD IT!
Design a farm vehicle. What can it do? How does it help the farmer?
Cozy! I'd love a nap!
The leftover stalks are useful, too. They're turned into straw for pets' beds.

Most fruit grows best in hot countries. These oranges are ripe and ready to be picked.

Bananas grow in bunches. Guess how big the biggest one was.

OK, one banana, two bananas, three . . .

It was 473 bananas! I'll show you . . .

Bananas are the number one fruit crop in the world—100 billion of them are eaten every year. How many do you eat?

Farmers don't just grow things for us to eat. Cotton farms grow cotton to make fabric, oil, and animal feed.
Read all about it! Tree farms are the best because they give us wood and paper.
I like flower power. Flower farms are so colorful.
OLD

A one-acre (4,047 m^2) cotton field can help make 325 pairs of jeans!

BUILD IT!

Design and build your own farm. What will you grow on your farm?

Build a LEGO® farm!

Use your stickers to create a fun day on the farm!

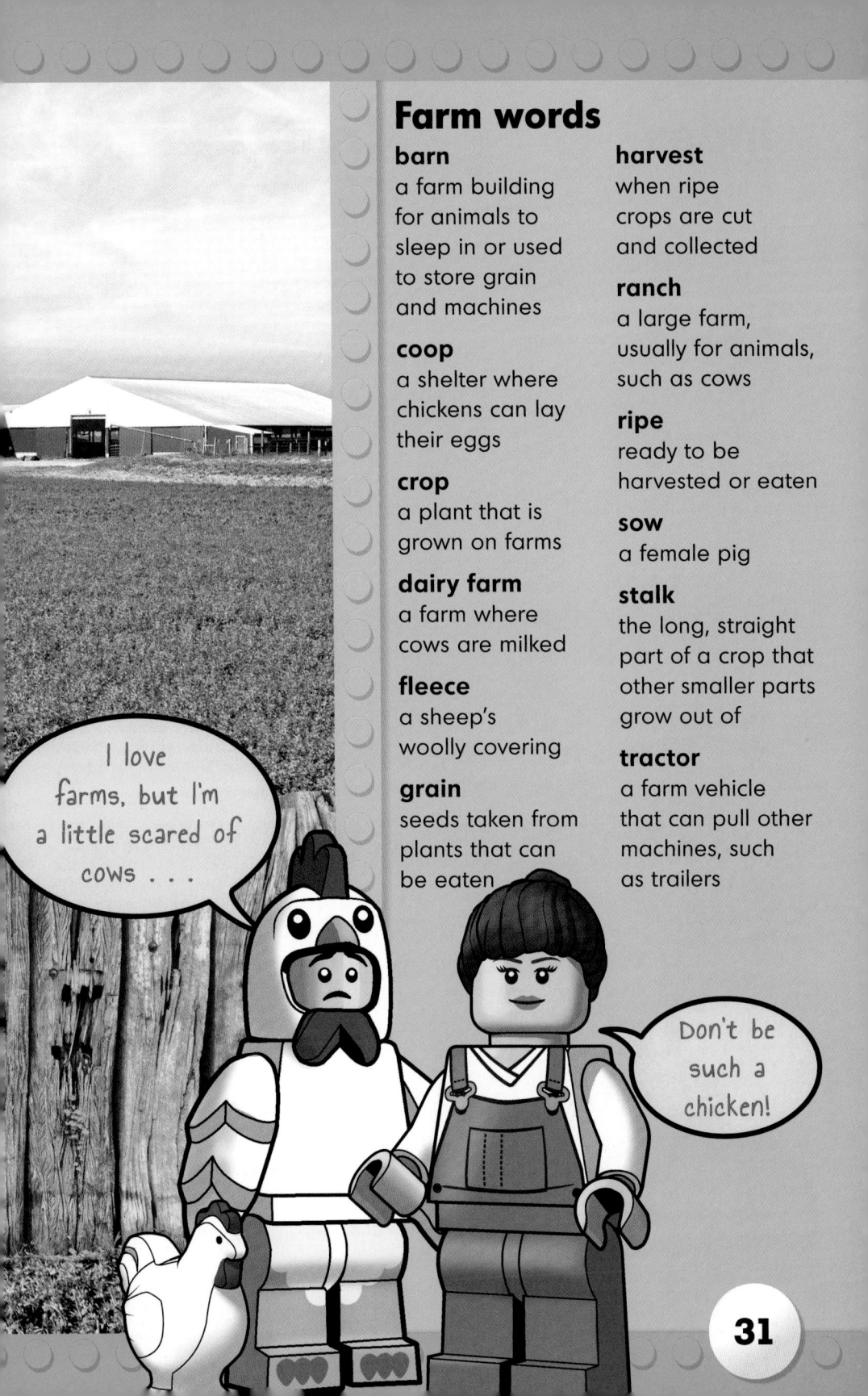

Farm words

barn
a farm building for animals to sleep in or used to store grain and machines

coop
a shelter where chickens can lay their eggs

crop
a plant that is grown on farms

dairy farm
a farm where cows are milked

fleece
a sheep's woolly covering

grain
seeds taken from plants that can be eaten

harvest
when ripe crops are cut and collected

ranch
a large farm, usually for animals, such as cows

ripe
ready to be harvested or eaten

sow
a female pig

stalk
the long, straight part of a crop that other smaller parts grow out of

tractor
a farm vehicle that can pull other machines, such as trailers

Index

A, B
apples 26
baler 21
bananas 27

C, D
chicken 6
chocolate 23
combine harvester 24
corn 22, 23
cotton 28
cows 10, 11, 12
cowboys
  and cowgirls 12, 13

E, F, G
eggs 6, 7
fleece 15, 17
frog 10
fruit 26
grain 24

H, I, J
jeans 29

K, L, M
lambs 14, 15
machine 20, 24
milk 8, 10, 11

N, O, P
oranges 26
pigs 8, 9
plow 20

Q, R, S
ranch 12
sheep 15, 16
sheepdog 16
sow 8
sprayer 21
straw 25

T, U, V
tire 18, 19, 29
tractor 5, 18, 19, 20
trailer 20

W, X, Y, Z
wheat 24
whistle 16
wool 17

Credits

For the LEGO Group: Randi Kirsten Sørensen *Licensing Assistant Manager*; Peter Moorby *Licensing Coordinator*; Heidi K. Jensen *Licensing Manager*

Photos ©: cover top: Stepanyda/iStockphoto; cover cow: mihtiander/iStockphoto; back cover top background: SADLERC1/iStockphoto; cover center background: MaxyM/Shutterstock; cover bottom background: StanRohrer/iStockphoto; back cover center: GaryAlvis/iStockphoto; 1: taxzi/iStockphoto; 2-3 top: ands456/iStockphoto; 3 sheep: sponner/iStockphoto; 4-5 top background: Maksymowicz/iStockphoto; 4 top: stefann11/iStockphoto; 5 top: agmit/iStockphoto; 6-7 top: FiledIMAGE/iStockphoto; 6-7 bottom background: wuttichok/iStockphoto; 6 bottom: anna1311/iStockphoto; 7 top right: georgeclerk/iStockphoto; 8-9 top: hadynyah/iStockphoto; 8 farmhouse: Kenneth_Keifer/iStockphoto; 8-9 bottom: ChrisAt/iStockphoto; 8-9 fence: wuttichok/iStockphoto; 10-11: Roy Riley/Alamy Images; 12-13 background: AnnaGreen/iStockphoto; 13 bottom: johnnya123/iStockphoto; 14 lambs: Award/iStockphoto; 14-15 field: blew_i/iStockphoto; 15 bottom: agmit/iStockphoto; 16-17 top background: Bigandt_Photography/iStockphoto; 16 bottom: annaia/iStockphoto; 16-17 stone wall: ands456/iStockphoto; 17 top right: sponner/iStockphoto; 18-19: Rihardzz/Shutterstock; 20-21 top: oticki/iStockphoto; 20 center left: deyanarobova/iStockphoto; 20 bottom: valio84sl/iStockphoto; 20 center right: Nerthuz/iStockphoto; 22-23 background: oticki/iStockphoto; 22 trailer: zorandimzr/iStockphoto; 22 bottom right: stoonn/iStockphoto; 22 top: Shinyfamily/iStockphoto; 22 bottom left: Lezh/iStockphoto; 24-25 top background: ThomasLENNE/Shutterstock; 24-25 bottom background: Igor Strukov/Shutterstock; 26 top left: MaIII Themd/Shutterstock; 26-27 background: apiguide/Shutterstock; 27 bottom right: aluxum/iStockphoto; 27 bottom left: loops7/iStockphoto; 28 center left: ithinksky/iStockphoto; 28 top left: PeteMuller/iStockphoto; 28-29 top background: Joobhead/iStockphoto; 29 jeans: Mehmet Hilmi Barcin/iStockphoto; 30 bottom left: anna1311/iStockphoto; 30-31 fence: wuttichok/iStockphoto; 30-31 top: stu99/iStockphoto.

All LEGO illustrations and stickers by Paul Lee

LEGO, the LEGO logo, the Minifigure, and the Brick and Knob configuration are trademarks and/or copyrights of the LEGO Group. All rights reserved.

©2018 The LEGO Group.

Manufactured by Scholastic Inc., 557 Broadway, New York, NY 10012 under license from the LEGO Group.

All rights reserved. Published by Scholastic Inc., *Publishers since 1920.* SCHOLASTIC and associated logos are trademarks and/or registered trademarks of Scholastic Inc.

The publisher does not have any control over and does not assume any responsibility for author or third-party websites or their content.

No part of this publication may be reproduced, stored in a retrieval system, or transmitted in any form or by any means, electronic, mechanical, photocopying, recording, or otherwise, without written permission of the publisher. For information regarding permission, write to Scholastic Inc., Attention: Permissions Department, 557 Broadway, New York, NY 10012.

ISBN 978-1-338-21424-6

10 9 8 7 6 5 4 3 2 18 19 20 21 22

Printed in the U.S.A. 40
First edition, January 2018

PO# 609481